light

A GUIDED JOURNAL THROUGH SCRIPTURE

My Word in 30 Days

HILLSEED
JOURNALS

LYNDSEY LINDSAY

COPYRIGHT ©2022 HILLSEED JOURNALS.
All rights reserved. No part of this book may be reproduced in any form without written permission from the publisher.
Do not replicate or copy.

ISBN 978-1-7377809-2-2

First paperback edition 2022.

Scripture quotations taken from the (NASB®) New American Standard Bible®, Copyright ©1960, 1971, 1977, 1995, 2020 by The Lockman Foundation. Used by permission. All rights reserved. www.lockman.org

All images ©Adobe Stock (stock.adobe.com). Used with license.

Copyright ©2011 The Montserrat Project Authors (https://github.com/JulietaUla/Montserrat). Used with permission.

Book cover design by The Book Cover Whisperer: ProfessionalBookCoverDesign.com

www.hillseedjournals.com

HOW TO USE THIS JOURNAL

We are so glad you are here!

The Bible is our most useful tool for getting to know who God is and His purpose for our lives, and we can't wait for you to do both.

The pages ahead are grouped into **three parts**, all designed to gently guide you through scripture and prompt you to **pursue the Holy Spirit in this journey over the next 30 days**.

1. Introduction..5

   Start by uncovering your big picture thoughts and ideas for the 30 days ahead that you will spend in scripture.

   You will also find a resource to introduce you to the major themes of the books of the Bible.

2. My Word in 30 Days..11

   Each day will introduce new scripture with consistent and guided journaling prompts.

3. Insights + Action..73

   After digging into *My Word in 30 Days*, you'll put it all together to uncover key biblical insights and faith-based action steps.

Let's grow our understanding of the Bible one day at a time.

For more information and resources:
visit **www.hillseedjournals.com**

introduction

The Lord is my light and my salvation;
whom shall I fear?
The Lord is the defense of my life;
whom shall I dread?

PSALM 27:1

Light is woven in God's story as a powerful symbol throughout the Old and New Testaments.

Over the next 30 days, you will explore how light appears throughout scripture—from the first words recorded by God, "Let there be light", to God's promise to appoint a "light to the nations", to Jesus' call to "Let your light shine before others".

No matter where you are in your faith, we have all experienced times when we open our Bibles and are unsure of where to start or had difficulty understanding scripture.

This is more than a Bible study. This is more than the word "light".

This is about creating confidence to read, reflect, and apply the Word to our lives every day.

LIGHT

What does light mean to you? Define the full meaning of light in your own words.

What do you want to learn about light over the next 30 days? Share your thoughts and ideas below.

RESOURCE | OLD TESTAMENT BOOK THEMES

LAW
Genesis
Exodus
Leviticus
Numbers
Deuteronomy

HISTORY
Joshua
Judges
Ruth
1 Samuel
2 Samuel
1 Kings
2 Kings
1 Chronicles
2 Chronicles
Ezra
Nehemiah
Esther

WISDOM
Job
Psalms
Proverbs
Ecclesiates
Song of Solomon

PROPHECY
Isaiah
Jeremiah
Lamentations
Ezekiel
Daniel
Hosea
Joel
Amos
Obadiah
Jonah
Micah
Nahum
Habakkuk
Zephaniah
Haggai
Zachariah
Malachi

NEW TESTAMENT BOOK THEMES

GOSPELS	Matthew
	Mark
	Luke
	John
HISTORY	Acts
LETTERS	Romans
	1 Corinthians
	2 Corinthians
	Galatians
	Ephesians
	Philippians
	Colossians
	1 Thessalonians
	2 Thessalonians
	1 Timothy
	2 Timothy
	Titus
	Philemon
	Hebrews
	James
	1 Peter
	2 Peter
	1 John
	2 John
	3 John
	Jude
PROPHECY	Revelation

TIP: *Use this resource to consider the major themes and context of the books of the Bible.*

my word in 30 days

Those who have insight
will shine brightly like the
brightness of the expanse of
heaven, and those who lead
the many to righteousness,
like the stars forever and ever.

DANIEL 12:3

DAY 1 | LIGHT

Pray over today's scripture, asking the Holy Spirit to lead you. Reread it and write what stands out in the space below.

GENESIS 1:1-18

Observe the text for context, teaching, and themes.

What is God revealing to you?

How can you apply this to your life today?

Prayer + Notes

DAY 2 | LIGHT

Pray over today's scripture, asking the Holy Spirit to lead you. Reread it and write what stands out in the space below.

2 SAMUEL 23:3-5

Observe the text for context, teaching, and themes.

What is God revealing to you?

How can you apply this to your life today?

Prayer + Notes

DAY 3 | LIGHT

Pray over today's scripture, asking the Holy Spirit to lead you. Reread it and write what stands out in the space below.

JOB 24:13-17

Observe the text for context, teaching, and themes.

What is God revealing to you?

How can you apply this to your life today?

Prayer + Notes

DAY 4 | LIGHT

Pray over today's scripture, asking the Holy Spirit to lead you. Reread it and write what stands out in the space below.

JOB 38:12-24

Observe the text for context, teaching, and themes.

What is God revealing to you?

How can you apply this to your life today?

Prayer + Notes

DAY 5 | LIGHT

Pray over today's scripture, asking the Holy Spirit to lead you. Reread it and write what stands out in the space below.

PSALM 36:5-9

Observe the text for context, teaching, and themes.

What is God revealing to you?

How can you apply this to your life today?

Prayer + Notes

DAY 6 | LIGHT

Pray over today's scripture, asking the Holy Spirit to lead you. Reread it and write what stands out in the space below.

PSALM 37

Observe the text for context, teaching, and themes.

What is God revealing to you?

How can you apply this to your life today?

Prayer + Notes

DAY 7 | LIGHT

Pray over today's scripture, asking the Holy Spirit to lead you. Reread it and write what stands out in the space below.

PROVERBS 4

Observe the text for context, teaching, and themes.

What is God revealing to you?

How can you apply this to your life today?

Prayer + Notes

DAY 8 | LIGHT

Pray over today's scripture, asking the Holy Spirit to lead you. Reread it and write what stands out in the space below.

ISAIAH 42:1-13

Observe the text for context, teaching, and themes.

What is God revealing to you?

How can you apply this to your life today?

Prayer + Notes

DAY 9 | LIGHT

Pray over today's scripture, asking the Holy Spirit to lead you. Reread it and write what stands out in the space below.

ISAIAH 50

Observe the text for context, teaching, and themes.

What is God revealing to you?

How can you apply this to your life today?

Prayer + Notes

DAY 10 | LIGHT

Pray over today's scripture, asking the Holy Spirit to lead you. Reread it and write what stands out in the space below.

ISAIAH 60

Observe the text for context, teaching, and themes.

What is God revealing to you?

How can you apply this to your life today?

Prayer + Notes

DAY 11 | LIGHT

Pray over today's scripture, asking the Holy Spirit to lead you. Reread it and write what stands out in the space below.

AMOS 5

Observe the text for context, teaching, and themes.

What is God revealing to you?

How can you apply this to your life today?

Prayer + Notes

DAY 12 | LIGHT

Pray over today's scripture, asking the Holy Spirit to lead you. Reread it and write what stands out in the space below.

PSALM 43

Observe the text for context, teaching, and themes.

What is God revealing to you?

How can you apply this to your life today?

Prayer + Notes

DAY 13 | LIGHT

Pray over today's scripture, asking the Holy Spirit to lead you. Reread it and write what stands out in the space below.

JOHN 1:1-18

Observe the text for context, teaching, and themes.

What is God revealing to you?

How can you apply this to your life today?

Prayer + Notes

DAY 14 | LIGHT

Pray over today's scripture, asking the Holy Spirit to lead you. Reread it and write what stands out in the space below.

MATTHEW 2:1-12

Observe the text for context, teaching, and themes.

What is God revealing to you?

How can you apply this to your life today?

Prayer + Notes

DAY 15 | LIGHT

Pray over today's scripture, asking the Holy Spirit to lead you. Reread it and write what stands out in the space below.

JOHN 3:1-21

Observe the text for context, teaching, and themes.

What is God revealing to you?

How can you apply this to your life today?

Prayer + Notes

DAY 16 | LIGHT

Pray over today's scripture, asking the Holy Spirit to lead you. Reread it and write what stands out in the space below.

MATTHEW 4:12-17

Observe the text for context, teaching, and themes.

What is God revealing to you?

How can you apply this to your life today?

Prayer + Notes

DAY 17 | LIGHT

Pray over today's scripture, asking the Holy Spirit to lead you. Reread it and write what stands out in the space below.

MATTHEW 5:13-20

Observe the text for context, teaching, and themes.

What is God revealing to you?

How can you apply this to your life today?

Prayer + Notes

DAY 18 | LIGHT

Pray over today's scripture, asking the Holy Spirit to lead you. Reread it and write what stands out in the space below.

LUKE 8:16-18, LUKE 11:33-36

Observe the text for context, teaching, and themes.

What is God revealing to you?

How can you apply this to your life today?

Prayer + Notes

DAY 19 | LIGHT

Pray over today's scripture, asking the Holy Spirit to lead you. Reread it and write what stands out in the space below.

MARK 4:1-25

Observe the text for context, teaching, and themes.

What is God revealing to you?

How can you apply this to your life today?

Prayer + Notes

DAY 20 | LIGHT

Pray over today's scripture, asking the Holy Spirit to lead you. Reread it and write what stands out in the space below.

JOHN 8

Observe the text for context, teaching, and themes.

What is God revealing to you?

How can you apply this to your life today?

Prayer + Notes

DAY 21 | LIGHT

Pray over today's scripture, asking the Holy Spirit to lead you. Reread it and write what stands out in the space below.

JOHN 12:12-50

Observe the text for context, teaching, and themes.

What is God revealing to you?

How can you apply this to your life today?

Prayer + Notes

DAY 22 | LIGHT

Pray over today's scripture, asking the Holy Spirit to lead you. Reread it and write what stands out in the space below.

ACTS 9:1-31

Observe the text for context, teaching, and themes.

What is God revealing to you?

How can you apply this to your life today?

Prayer + Notes

DAY 23 | LIGHT

Pray over today's scripture, asking the Holy Spirit to lead you. Reread it and write what stands out in the space below.

ACTS 12:1-19

Observe the text for context, teaching, and themes.

What is God revealing to you?

How can you apply this to your life today?

Prayer + Notes

DAY 24 | LIGHT

Pray over today's scripture, asking the Holy Spirit to lead you. Reread it and write what stands out in the space below.

2 CORINTHIANS 4

Observe the text for context, teaching, and themes.

What is God revealing to you?

How can you apply this to your life today?

Prayer + Notes

DAY 25 | LIGHT

Pray over today's scripture, asking the Holy Spirit to lead you. Reread it and write what stands out in the space below.

EPHESIANS 5:1-21

Observe the text for context, teaching, and themes.

What is God revealing to you?

How can you apply this to your life today?

Prayer + Notes

DAY 26 | LIGHT

Pray over today's scripture, asking the Holy Spirit to lead you. Reread it and write what stands out in the space below.

PSALM 119:129-136

Observe the text for context, teaching, and themes.

What is God revealing to you?

How can you apply this to your life today?

Prayer + Notes

DAY 27 | LIGHT

Pray over today's scripture, asking the Holy Spirit to lead you. Reread it and write what stands out in the space below.

1 JOHN 1

Observe the text for context, teaching, and themes.

What is God revealing to you?

How can you apply this to your life today?

Prayer + Notes

DAY 28 | LIGHT

Pray over today's scripture, asking the Holy Spirit to lead you. Reread it and write what stands out in the space below.

REVELATION 21

Observe the text for context, teaching, and themes.

What is God revealing to you?

How can you apply this to your life today?

Prayer + Notes

DAY 29 | LIGHT

Pray over today's scripture, asking the Holy Spirit to lead you. Reread it and write what stands out in the space below.

REVELATION 22

Observe the text for context, teaching, and themes.

What is God revealing to you?

How can you apply this to your life today?

Prayer + Notes

DAY 30 | LIGHT

Pray over today's scripture, asking the Holy Spirit to lead you. Reread it and write what stands out in the space below.

PSALM 139:7-12

Observe the text for context, teaching, and themes.

What is God revealing to you?

How can you apply this to your life today?

Prayer + Notes

insights + action

Your word is a lamp to my feet and a light to my path.

PSALM 119:105

INSIGHTS | LIGHT

Let's revisit the last 30 days! Consider and meditate on your last 30 days spent in the Word of God and in prayer. Identify key insights about light from the Holy Spirit and capture them below.

ACTION | LIGHT

Now let's turn your insights into faith-based action steps!

Draw/write what comes to mind. Be as specific as possible.

> **TIP**: *For a starting point, review your life application notes from days 1–30.*

LIGHT

We are celebrating and praising God for the progress you have made in this journey. Whatever that may look like for you, you did it!

Redefine the full meaning of light in your own words, using your newly-gained, biblical insight.

Who can you share this with?

From the end of the earth I call to You when my heart is faint; Lead me to the rock that is higher than I.

PSALM 61:2

Get your new journal at
hillseedjournals.com

www.ingramcontent.com/pod-product-compliance
Lightning Source LLC
Chambersburg PA
CBHW041309110526
44590CB00028B/4303